WHERE'S MY OTHER SOCK?

WHERE'S MY OTHER SOCK?

DO'S, DON'TS & THINK ABOUT'S FOR
YOUNG MEN MOVING OUT OF HOME

LEANNE KOSTER

ISBN 978-0-646-81808-5

Contributions by Jordan Koster
Illustrations by Toby Bridson

FOR JAKE

May your corn kernels always have a cob
and your stuffing be filled with walnuts.

CONGRATS ON THE BIG MOVE

So, you've decided that it's time to venture out on your own, to take that leap of independence. Time to find out what it's really like to live out of home. Time to party like there is no tomorrow. Perhaps you're excited, or perhaps this feels less like a decision and more like a scary, unavoidable step.

However you're feeling, this quick guide for young men will help with the moving out of home process.

Either way… CONGRATS!

The thought of doing what you want, when you want, how you want and with whomever the hell you want, is incredibly appealing. There may just be a teeny-weeny bit of fear as well, which is perfectly normal.

You may be wondering, will you have enough money to eat the way you did at home? Or you may have already accepted your new diet could very well consist of 2-minute noodles or bread and vegemite (no butter because it's too expensive).

Your skills in the kitchen may range from "which one is the spatula?" to "I find a gentle sauté brings out the best flavor in Bokchoy." If you think you could replace that home-cooked delicious lasagna or grandma's to-die-for apple crumble, then you're probably ahead of me in the kitchen game.

And if you already know the difference between legs, shoulders, rolled and butterflied pieces of meat – go you! You may not even need this book.

If this sounds like gibberish to you, you may like a bit of a life line. Read on and let's see if we can make staying afloat a bit easier for you.

It is important that you know this is not a cook book. There are hundreds, no, thousands of them online and on every bookstore shelf, all written by people who actually have a passion for cooking. I however, do not. I would rather run naked around a football field on Grand Final Day than be stuck in the kitchen over a hot stove (just ask my family). But we all know eating out every night is neither practical nor affordable.

So, I thought I'd give you a few shortcuts. Smart, simple options will have you in, and more importantly, out, of the kitchen in the shortest time possible. Or if you love cooking, then my address is in the back of the book – does five o'clock work for you?

We'll take care of your stomach later on – there are a few other things that need to be addressed as part of stepping into the adult world. Finding a house or flat, going it alone or having housemates, furniture, appliances and of course the big one… bills. You are probably thinking to yourself – "yeah yeah, I know what I'm doing. I've had a part time job for years and I've been paying my own way". But I do have to ask the question – does paying your own way mean you fork out for your boozy nights out and the odd pizza or does it mean you've been paying for electricity, house and contents insurance, phone bills and rent?

If that all sounds new and difficult, not to worry. Read on and learn.

WHERE TO LIVE

Finding a place to live can be as simple as looking on the internet for something affordable and putting in an application, but there are a few things that you might also want to consider. For example, the rent might be cheap, but it could be in a super dodgy area full of criminals who have their eye on your laptop (which you leave on your desk by the front window in plain view). Also, the money that you save on rent might disappear on fuel for your car if the house is a long way from work, uni or friends and family.

Here are a few other useful questions to ask yourself:

Is it close to public transport? This is important for those of you who don't have a car.

What's the neighborhood like? Do you feel safe? Feeling safe is as important for you guys as it is for girls.

How far is it from friends, uni, work, gym, shops, parents, a good pizza place and your favourite bars?

Is there off-street parking? If so, how may car spots?

What's your phone reception like? There is nothing worse than moving somewhere and not having good phone reception. Trust me, I made that costly mistake midway through a two-year prepaid plan.

DOLLARS FOR THE BIG MOVE

It's all well and good to make the big decision to move out of home, but are you clear on what it will cost? I'm sure it's more than likely that your guardians have been paying for a lot of house stuff that you didn't even know existed before now. The electricity powering your game consoles and the free-flowing internet isn't magic, you know. It has to be connected and it costs money – every single month, every year, forever.

You will need to save a not-so-small pile of cash to get stuff connected in the beginning and then to keep stuff running.

Firstly, you will need a rental bond. This is usually one month of rent, put aside by the real estate agent as insurance against you trashing the place. Once you move out, if everything is clean and in one piece then you will get this money back. Seriously try to keep the place intact, because getting your bond back is a good safety net for paying the bond of the next place you move to. The really bad news - you'll need to pay one month's rent for bond plus one month's rent in advance. It's a bugger you have to pay for something before you use it, but unfortunately that's the way it is. But wait, there's more…

- Electricity, water, gas, phone – all need to be connected which usually means a connection fee. This varies from provider to provider so make sure you shop around.

- Food and grocery costs. I'll cover this more later but it's not just food that you will be forking out for, it is cleaning products, washing powder etc.

- Furniture – when I first moved out I begged, borrowed (but did not steal) as much as I could. There were no matching plates or bowls in our house. No fancy knives and forks and no expensive gadgets. Secondhand anything and everything was the game and we got really good at playing it. After all, there was partying to be done and better places to spend our hard-earned cash. Op shops, eBay and family are a great place to start for these household essentials.

- If you have a car, have you taken into account fuel, insurance, registration, servicing, repairs and the odd parking fine?

- Ambulance subscription – an odd addition to this list I know but an important one. It costs less than $50 a year. You have probably been on your parent's ambulance policy until now but once you are over 18 you are no longer automatically covered. I discovered this after my son had a costly trip to the hospital. He was lucky in more ways than one –he was physically ok, and the ambulance bill was only $700. I say "only", because it could have been up to $5,000, and that is not something you want to be paying when you have other expenses and bills to think about!

TO SHARE OR NOT TO SHARE

It's more than likely you are sharing a house with others in order to keep your expenses down - probably mates but possibly strangers you met on the internet. It's essential that you decide on some ground rules from day one about how you want to handle things like cooking, bills, visitors and cleaning the toilet. More about cleaning later; let's start with food.

From a budget point of view, it's much cheaper to pool your money, buy in bulk and cook together instead of doing it on your own. This of course depends on your personal food tastes and whether they differ too much from your housemates'. If you are all pretty similar or happy to at least work together then here is my suggestion based on there being three of you. For more or less bodies, just adjust accordingly.

Sit down together and work out how much you want to spend on food each week. This will help to determine whether you have steak for dinner every night, cheap pasta dishes or a mixture of the two. Make sure you are all on the same page. If not, it's ok to go it alone food wise.

If you all agree on the share option, then have each person write a list of at least five of their favourite meals. Hint – if you are all pretty busy with sport, work and dating/partners then include things like pasta, rice and slow-cooker casseroles into your lists. Don't worry about the how to do them, I will get to that later.

- Combine the lists and then cross out any of the meals that you would not all be happy to eat. This helps form your basic meal plan.

- Decide how many nights a week you'll eat together (this doesn't mean you have to eat at the same time, but it does mean you'll be eating the same food). Select one or two nights per week that each person will cook, taking into account who has what social and sporting commitments each night. As most of you are out and about on weekends, I suggest Friday and Saturday nights be left as "fend for yourself" nights – it tends to work out better for everyone if you're all going to end up getting an HSP on your way home from a big night out – extra cheese, of course.

- Split your fridge up so that you have shared areas as well as individual shelves/spots for your own special treats. This is particularly important for when partners who don't live in the house show up wanting a feed. Tupperware containers can be useful for this and can be labeled easily so there is no confusion. I've never had to resort to plugging a mini-fridge into my room, but I've been pretty lucky with housemates.

- Write a shopping list of all the "share" things you need for that week to make the agreed meals and manage the day-to-day running of your house. For brekky, lunch and snacks, decide on who wants what and add these staples to your list. Don't forget to include things like butter, milk, sugar, coffee, tea, spices, sauces, condiments (meaning jam, vegemite, honey).

Budgeting can be tricky in a share house as individual earnings can vary quite a lot, and everyone has different priorities when it comes to what they want to spend their money on. There is no "right" answer here, but one option is that each of you put $50 into a kitty (aka tin on the fridge) to cover shared items. Things like toilet paper, cleaning products, toothpaste, milk or anything else that you agree should be in this list. When the kitty runs dry, you put in another $50 each and so on. Some shared houses I've lived in take it in turns each week, but I have found this is harder to manage (and not always fair) as you don't always need to buy dishwashing detergent each week.

While the thought of a share house is super exciting to you right now, the novelty will wear off at some stage (probably around week four) and reality will kick in, so here are a few things to keep in mind.

Sharing can be tough. I know that you are not toddlers anymore and that your parents have probably done a brilliant job of teaching you to share, but it is a whole different ball game when it comes to sharing with your housemates. And while I am going to only be focusing on the sharing of food and kitchen stuff, the rules of sharing can and should apply to just about everything – make sure your partners know these house rules too!

Communication is VITAL! If things aren't working the way you would like, then you have to talk about it, preferably before things blow completely out of proportion and you all go running home to your respective carers (if they haven't already turned your bedroom into a yoga studio that is).

Set clear rules and have them displayed on the fridge or in a prominent place in the house. I know this sounds like hard work or even worse, like you are back at school but the clearer everyone is about both individual and group expectations, the smoother it will be for all of you.

LIVING WITH GIRLS

You may have chosen to share a house with guys or girls or a mixture of the two, but either way, I wanted to give you a little heads-up about living with girls. For those of you who grew up with sisters then you are already a step ahead, but please remember that living with girls who are not biologically related to you is NOT the same. They don't have to love you no matter what, and I promise you, they won't.

The following tips are designed for your own protection. Feel free to ignore these suggestions but do so at your own peril.

IN THE KITCHEN

Please do not assume that all girls know how to cook and/or like it. And if you value your life, do not suggest that a girl's natural place is in the kitchen (or the laundry for that matter). Remember sharp knives are kept in there as well and she will not be afraid to use them – and not for chopping your veggies!

IN THE BATHROOM

If you are living with girls please do not, no matter how much of a hurry you are in, urinate with the seat down. Sitting down to pee on a damp seat is… seriously there are just no words (or at least none that can be included if I am to have any hope of getting this published).

If it is your turn to clean the bathroom, wipe the walls, the floors, under the toilet, behind the toilet, around the base, inside the toilet.

Do not be afraid to use extra cleaning product. (Side note – I suggest chemical free, environmentally friendly products as sitting down on a seat just washed with bleach or some of the harsher products out there is not much fun).

If your shaved hair lands on a surface, wipe it off.

Empty toilet rolls. Take them off and put a new one on. It's that simple! Make it easy by having a bin next to the toilet so you don't have to exert too much additional energy. I know you'll need that later for getting drinks from the fridge or ordering UberEats.

PERIODS

Do not assume that a bad mood is because of her period. Let me say it again: do NOT assume that her bad mood is because of her period. One more time for the guys at the back? No, I think you get the picture. She might just be hungry, frustrated with an assignment, or her housemate (not looking at anyone in particular) could be acting like an idiot.

And do not, under ANY circumstances, blame her mood on her period out loud. Think it if you must, but silence is the best option here. Yes, hormones make us act in ways we may not otherwise, but often it's a matter of something very real finally coming to the surface because our fuse has been shortened by the strain our body is under for days on end. A bit of perspective and kindness can go a long way.

Cramps hurt. Not all girls have them but for some it is like some nasty Basilisk, Demogorgon, or just your everyday goblin (pick your pop-culture poison) is ripping your insides out with a sharp, serrated knife.

Add a rainbow of emotions ranging from sad crying, happy crying or even angry crying (yes, it's a thing) and you still haven't got a clue. So yes, there's a good chance there will be a lot of tears.

Offerings of chocolate, a warm heat-pack or a nice cup of tea (or vodka), will be greatly appreciated and will most likely earn you credits that can be cashed in for favours at some later stage.

Consider, just for a moment, the possibility that her shitty mood is just because you keep leaving empty toilet rolls on the holder and the seat up! Or whatever… Not because of her period.

LIVING ON CAMPUS

While I did live on campus when I went to uni, it was a long time and many wines ago, so I am handing over to someone who is living the dream right now – my super awesome daughter who is drinking (I mean studying conscientiously) through her first year of uni.

Over to you honey…

So first off, Mum did not mean "studying conscientiously" and we all know it. I'm now on my 10th month on college and I think I need a new liver. If anyone is offering, please hit me up.

But anyway, moving onto the important stuff.

If you think moving to college is the same as moving into a house or apartment, you are horribly mistaken. All of those stereotypes about university and how crazy first year is, come from those in their first year. Don't fool yourself into thinking you will sleep for the first six months. Don't make the mistake of thinking you won't become a low-key alcoholic in the first couple of weeks (or a high-key alcoholic in the last couple of weeks of semester, you know, that time all those assignments are due). O-Week is a crazy, fun, messy week you're unlikely to remember. College will be the craziest experience you've had, and if you're anything like me, a handy how-to guide would have been useful in preparation.

So, without further ado, I am going to give you some helpful hints on how to survive living on College.

MOVING IN

Moving day is nerve-wracking; there's no hiding it. You are about to move into a building with around 80 other people from all around the country and around the world who are just as nervous as you are. It was probably the best and worst day in my college experience, but here's how you get through it.

Move in on the earliest possible date. This isn't a requirement, but it makes everything a whole lot easier. I could move in on the 11th of February, so I arrived on the 11th of February. It was awesome to know everyone was in the same boat; it was everyone's first day and we were all getting used to living away from home together. A few of my mates moved in days or weeks later and regretted it. They said they felt everyone had their groups of friends already, so it was even more intimidating for them.

However, if you have commitments that prevent you from doing so, don't worry. Just keep in mind everyone has no idea what they're doing. Those kids who have been there from day one are faking it. Sure, they may know how to use the kitchen, they might have a couple of people they feel comfortable enough to call "friends", but they're almost as new to the experience as you are. Be confident. Talk to them. That's how you fit in.

WHAT TO BRING

If you are likely to go home often, don't take everything. Take what you need (i.e. toiletries, technology, food, clothes etc.) but don't pack anything unnecessary. You don't know how much space you have in your room, and you don't want to be freaking out about not enough storage on your first day.

If you are from interstate/overseas, TAKE EVERYTHING. Okay, maybe not everything, but as much as you can fit into your bags. Remember, you are not around the corner. You can't call your mum and say, "I forgot all my shoes, can you come drop them off?" Because she can't. It's at least a flight, and sometimes oceans away.

Also, learn from my mistakes. When you're moving out, you're not thinking about school. You're thinking about dorm-life, if you'll meet anyone cool, if you'll get in the shower in the communal bathroom and then realise you left your towel on your bed.

All I can say is, you need textbooks. Don't do what I did and forget to take pens, pencils and notebooks. Sure, you'll use your laptop a lot, but you still need pens.

MAKING FRIENDS

It's not that simple, I know. I sucked at talking to new people. Up until I moved out, my awesome mum and author of this book was still making appointments to the hairdresser for me. It's what made me the most nervous about moving out, but it's the only way to survive. Your mantra should be "everyone is in the same boat", so they're hoping you'll talk to them just as much as you're hoping they'll talk to you. It's like trying to hook up at a club. You're looking at each other hoping the other will come up to your first. Man up and make the first move. Here are some questions you'll ask and answer a million times, but they're good to know.

- Where are you from?
- What are you studying?
- What High School did you go to?
- Did you take a Gap Year? (If so, where did you go?)
- Do you work? (If so, what do you do?)

- Do you like travel/have you travelled much?
- Do you speak other languages?
- Do you play sports?

You get the picture. Get to know them, and I promise you will be friends for at least 24 hours. That's enough time to make new friends if you don't like their answers to the above questions.

COOKING GROUPS

If you are living in dorm-style accommodation, it is a good idea to make a cooking group. This just means that one day a week, each member in the group cooks a meal for everyone to share. It not only saves money that can be put to better use (and I think we all know what I'm talking about), it is a good way to try new foods and make friends. There are only a couple of rules:

- Make your cooking group with people who like similar foods. Spicy, bland, complex, basic: it makes or breaks a cooking group

- Have a limit on meals so that everyone is spending the same amount. We usually had a cap of $20, otherwise it can get messy when you realize you are forking out $40 per meal, while others are only paying $15.

- Four people is the maximum I would recommend for cooking groups. That covers dinners from Monday to Thursday, leaving the weekends to fend for yourselves. It's easier this way, trust me.

Cooking groups aren't for everyone, but if you're up for having a good time cooking with some new friends, and saving cash, I would recommend it.

HELPFUL HINTS

College life comes with its challenges, particularly when living with so many new and different people. There are so many things you won't be prepared for, so I thought I'd give you a bit of a heads up on how to deal with some inevitable situations.

- Bathrooms: they are communal, and sometimes unisex, so be sure to clean up after yourself to avoid drama

- Drinking: drinking is great, and it's something almost everyone participates in. Notice how I said "almost"? Some people don't like it, don't want to be a part of it, and that's okay. It doesn't mean you can't drink, it just means to be respectful and if they ask you to turn the volume down because it's 3am and they have a lecture at 8am, maybe move onto another location and keep the party going.

- Studying: you need to do it. You're at uni for a reason, but that doesn't mean you'll make it to your 8am lectures on a Wednesday morning, when Tuesday's are uni night at the local pub. I certainly didn't go to all my lectures, but if you can't go, make sure you catch up. It saves many all-nighters, reduces finals week stress, and is way better for your mental health in the long run, too.

A final note: the college lifestyle many experience in their first year of uni is incredible; it is so full of new experiences and great people and almost too many nights of near-alcohol poisoning. If you are respectful of your neighbours and your uni residence's codes of conduct (boring, I know, but give it a quick read before moving in), you will have one of the best years of your life. Just remember that everyone is different, peer-pressure is never okay, and the more you participate in college events, the more you will get out of the year. Back to you mumma dearest…

ASKING FOR HELP

I am pretty confident that you guys are a whole lot smarter than some of the previous generations and know that the hide-your-feelings, I-got-this, I-don't-need-help, kind of bravado is no longer an essential ingredient of manhood. Not that it ever was, mind you.

Moving out can be a big deal. Don't be afraid (or too stubborn) to ask for help if you are struggling. Those first few months or even first year can be tough and there is no-one on the planet who is expecting you to get it right first up. NO-ONE! Especially not your guardians who have done it themselves. You think moving out is a tough gig – try parenting. But NOT YET! There is plenty of time for sowing seeds or whatever they call it these days.

Now is the time for having fun, trying to make the best decisions you can (at least some of the time) and making memories that will amuse your grandkids one day. But NOT YET! Unless of course you are 38 years old and reading this, then yes, NOW would be good.

TO INSURE OR NOT TO INSURE

Firstly, a brief lesson on insurance, just in case like me when I moved out the first time, you have no idea. When it comes to houses there is house insurance which covers the building itself and is covered by your landlord, unless you own the house then it is your responsibility. There is also contents insurance which covers everything inside the house; these are the things you bring to it – your furniture, laptops, phones, clothes, TVs etc.

It is easy to look at your possibly smallish, inexpensive list of belongings and wonder whether or not contents insurance is necessary. After all, insurance can cost quite a lot each year and you have other things like, oh you know – *eating* to budget for.

Of course, it's up to you, but from someone who was in a shared house of five when we were robbed, without insurance, it really sucked. We didn't have mobiles or laptops at that stage (okay, I am a little older than you guys but still oh so young in my mind), but between us we lost multiple music playing devices, our beloved microwave, several TVs and other bits and pieces that added up to a lot. It was the last time I lived in a house without contents insurance.

These days, considering how many electronic devices we all own, I think it is a bit of a must. Shop around and you will find a policy that will cover what you need but not eat into your social-life budget too much.

IN CASE OF EMERGENCIES

An emergency in your world may be that it is 4am and the pizza shop closed five minutes before you got there, and you are in desperate need of something to soak up the hours of $10 jugs that seemed like a good idea at happy hour. While I am going to leave you to navigate your own way through these types of emergencies, I will help out with some others you might face.

PERSONAL EMERGENCIES

Have a list of each of your housemate's emergency contact numbers. Parents/guardians, doctors - anyone that should be contacted if something was to happen to one of you.

If any of you have medical conditions like asthma or epilepsy, make sure appropriate first aid action plans are in a place where everyone can see them. It's simple but so incredibly important – make sure you are prepared so you can have each other's backs.

HOUSE EMERGENCIES

I have flooded two of the many houses I have lived in. Both quite badly and both which required a cry for outside help. The first time it happened, we were in our brand new, few-weeks-old, really really new house. Did I say it was my beautiful new house? I decided to soak some whites in a bucket in the laundry sink. I ran the tap (hot water) and then got distracted and went to finish cooking dinner. By the time I heard the running water sound it was too late. The bucket, which was covering the sink hole, filled and overflowed, filling the entire sink, which overflowed as well. Onto the laundry floor, out into the carpeted hallway.

After my screaming/sobbing subsided, made worse by the fact that this avoidable disaster was my fault, I was straight onto the phone to a friend because I had no idea what to do and I was pretty sure that I had already caused a bucket load of damage that would have a large repair bill attached to it. Thankfully she had done this before as well and told me there were professional clean up companies for this. A quick call to one saw them on my doorstep within the hour with huge industrial blowers. These magic fans sucked the water from the carpet and saved us from a bill with a few extra zeros on the end of it.

The second time was a forgotten hose that should have been attached to the sink so waste water could go down the drain. It wasn't me. Hubby this time. Every blanket, towel, sheet and pillow case in the house was used to try and mop up this disaster. Thankfully tiled floors meant no need for outside help.

The moral of this story… have a list of emergency numbers on your fridge. Include flood disaster companies, plumbers (a blocked loo can go badly very quickly) and electricians. As an electrician's daughter, I cannot emphasize this enough - DO NOT attempt to handle any electrical faults yourself – EVER! I promise you – if you are strapped for cash, ask your parents for some help as they would rather pay this bill than the one for your medical care (or worse).

THE SPARE KEY

I know you have you're an adult now but when it comes to locking yourself out of the house, age and experience doesn't come into it. We have all done it, and most of us more than once.

But there is a simple solution and it doesn't involve burying a key inside an old can in the backyard. While this is a perfectly viable solution, there is a damn good chance that you will forget where in the backyard you hid it, particularly when you have stumbled home in the middle of the night after one too many Jagers and are unable to find the zip in your jeans, let alone the buried treasure that will give you access to your much-needed bed.

There are these wonderful things called *key safes* or *spare key lock boxes*. They are a little box that attaches to something fixed outside your house like a water meter or post (anything that cannot be picked up and moved). These boxes are exactly like bike locks and have a three to four digit code that you set. You then put your key into the box, close it and mess up the digits so it no longer shows your access code. When you next lock yourself out of the house, your spare key will be right there, safely hidden away and waiting for you.

Now a couple of important things to remember:

Yes, one of them is the code itself. Don't be predictable and have the code be 0000 or 1234 or something that invites potential thieves into your home. You may as well just leave the front door open and have a six-pack of cold beers on the bench for would-be criminal.

Once you have needed to use the spare key (and believe me, you will), REMEMBER to put it back in the safe box so it is there for next time (and yes – there will be one of those too).

In case it isn't obvious already – make sure your housemates all have the code and make sure that you all agree about who else (if anyone) gets given the code. Partners, mates, parents, random strangers you meet in bars or clubs?

Just remember, relationships can go south, mates can become non-mates, parents can be invasive and random strangers you meet in bars, well, do I really need to spell that one out for you. Ultimately, it's pretty simple - the less people who know the code, the better.

ACCEPTABLE HOUSE BEHAVIOUR
(AKA THE RULES)

You and your mates may have thought that having your own place
meant wooohooooo, party time 24/7, and none of those stupid
restrictions that your parents put on you when living under *their* roof.
And it could mean that, and it probably will mean that for the first little
while. That is until the pure high of doing whatever you want, whenever
you want, wears off. Like when, for the third week in a row, *insert-
housemate-name-here*, refuses to wash his dishes and plays classical
music full blast till 4am every morning.

You can either do this next step before you decide who you are going to live with, when you first move in together or after the shit hits the fan – your call. Either way, make sure you are all on the same page when it comes to things like smoking, drinking, parties, swearing, guests, sharing, girlfriends/boyfriends, music, (particularly people who play instruments – drums, electric guitars, bagpipes!) Actually, if you have a bagpipe playing friend I'm thinking that you might want to rethink your taste in housemates, just maybe?

You don't need a formal list stuck to the fridge or anything carved in stone but be straight with each other about what you like and don't like. You can only put up with crap for a certain amount of time before it will push you over the edge. It is not worth losing great mates over, so better out than in I say.

So just on the whole *guest* thing.

I am guessing that it's safe to say you are probably not going to have your parents come stay over so I don't need to cover off anything there. But I do have something to say about managing the other common house guests who overstay their welcome. You know, the girlfriends/boyfriends/partners/mates who seem to have accidentally moved in without you knowing it.

These seemingly innocent offenders are easily identified by the one thing they all have in common. Can you guess what that is? Yep – they all live at home with their parents. They see you as their golden ticket to freedom – without any of the financial commitment. They get all the perks without any of the responsibility – it doesn't really get any better than that does it?

It's important for you and your actual housemates (the rent paying ones) to figure out how you want to handle situations like this. Ideally, you will have set some ground rules about this sort of thing when you first moved in together. And if not, I really do understand. You were so excited about the prospect of living in a house without rules, that it never even crossed your mind.

I wish I could tell you there is an easy solution. But there isn't. Well at least not one that won't involve some potentially tough conversations with both your paying and nonpaying housemates. But they are conversations you will need to have, if you want this whole house sharing business to work.

CLEANING THE HOUSE
(INSERT GROAN HERE)

I totally understand if you close this book now; I hate it, too. But it is, unfortunately, another requirement of living in a house that makes me wish I was still that innocent little four-year-old who had no understanding of what a scrubbing brush and toilet cleaner were. It was perfectly acceptable for the cleaning to be mum's job. Note, I would have said mum or dad's job, but I grew up in a time where lots of mums stayed home and handled everything to do with the house, including cleaning, and the dads went off to paid work.

If you can't afford a cleaner and your mum is not willing to come do it for you each week (which I hope to God that she isn't because she deserves a life of her own now she has finished raising you!) then you will need these tips.

I don't recommend sharing everything (partners are generally a no-go zone, as is the expensive bottle of rum that you got for your 18th birthday), however cleaning is definitely on the "shit we have to do together" list! Put together a rotating roster so one week you are lumped with the super disgusting cleaning jobs and other weeks you have slightly more pleasant tasks like vacuuming or dusting.

Here is a list of the things that need to be cleaned each week, in order of urgency. Don't freak out, it won't take you that long.

TOILETS

The nature of our bodily functions means that no matter what, these tiny rooms get gross really quickly. I suggest having a bottle of toilet cleaner and a brush beside each toilet for easy access. At least once per week give the entire bowl a good scrub, inside and out, including the top of the seat, under the seat, around the base and if necessary, the nearby walls. Also have a rubbish bin in each toilet so that empty toilet rolls can be disposed of without you having to exert too much energy. You and I both know that as soon as you have to go out of your way to throw it out, it's probably not going to happen.

BATHROOMS

Showers can get a build-up of mould and grime and other unknown matter quicker than the last craft beer a guest left behind from your house warming disappears.

VACUUMING

There is a machine for this that makes it quick and easy when done without heaving sighing or groaning. Plug end of lead into wall, hold onto long straight handle, turn power on and wander aimlessly around the house collecting dirt and dust. You will need to move stuff like couches to capture the pizza crusts that have mysteriously made their way underneath. Note – the furniture moving is not a requirement for house cleaning as you could go with the "what you can't see won't hurt you" style. However, if you choose this, be prepared for the additional house guests that will soon visit. They are small, furry, love food scraps and once they've moved in, are a little hard to get rid of. I personally prefer the short-term pain of cleaning to these pesky little critters.

KITCHEN

I am a fan of "clean as you go" when it comes to the kitchen but a weekly mop of the floors or at least a vacuum is worthwhile. A regular clean out of the fridge to remove the leftovers that you were sure you'd have tomorrow (a month ago) means that you won't have to throw out the entire container as greeny-brown stuff starts seeping out from the edges. When it comes to cleaning the stove, I'm not sure I can help you as my preferred philosophy is when it gets too dirty it's time to move to a new house or buy a new stove. Of course, neither of these are very practical, so let's just clean the stove.

BEDROOMS

Each person should be responsible for their own room. Clean, don't clean – it's up to each of you but remember that while you may be immune to your own stench, your friends, girlfriends/boyfriends and family are not. That's all I have to say on that.

CLEANING PRODUCTS

ALDI is my preferred store for cheap but good cleaning products (for the entire house) and cheap toilet paper that won't have your butt feels like it's being attacked by sandpaper. If you are environmentally aware then look for green products and spend a few extra dollars if you can. There is a great online company called EcoWorx which has chemical free products. They do cost a bit but are worth it. They make cleaning easy plus there are no strong smells of bleach left in your shower for hours, making it impossible for you to breathe, let alone bathe properly.

A FINAL WORD ON CLEANING

Unless you are one of those rare people who get off on cleaning (I wouldn't have believed it myself unless I had seen it with my own eyes), cleaning is unavoidable and necessary. The only way around it is to become financially successful and employ a cleaner but until that happens, remember: many hands make light work.

THIS IS THE WAY WE WASH OUR CLOTHES

Whites, darks, colours, hot, cold, gentle, delicate, spin, regular or permanent press. I get it - I lost you at whites. These are, however, some of the different cycles that you will see on a washing machine. You know, that machine that sits in the one room of the house you most likely didn't even know existed. That room where your dirty, smelly (yes – your stale, deodorant saturated body stench is not pretty) disappear into, only to magically return all clean and fresh and ready to wear. This 'magic' is the result of someone else's hard work!

It's up to you to make the magic happen now. Laundry and cleaning may seem mundane and boring. Once you've lived out of home for a while you'll realise there's nothing quite as magical as having a clean space to live in (and bring people home to).

Washing is pretty simple, and the fact that you are unlikely to have any 'delicates' (bra's, lacy undies and the like – or maybe you do – I'm not judging) makes it even easier.

I suggest you have a washing basket. Compared with leaving your shit strewn all over your bedroom floor, it will really help. If you can afford to have two baskets, even better – one for whites, one for all colours other than white. Except red! If you own anything red, you need to know that it must be treated like a prospective partner you're trying to impress. You don't just throw them in with your other things.

They are special, unique and need to be handled gently with lots of love and attention. And if you don't look after them as you should, boy will you know about it. They will turn all your other items a dirty shade of pink. Not a lovely, this-guy-is-really-secure-in-himself type of pink, but a motley ugly shade that will be relegated to the bottom of your wardrobe or to the Vinnies donation pile.

Whites can include pale greys if they have been washed before – they will not infect one another in any way. Your darks can include browns, blacks, blues and other colours; however, please please please remember that the first time you wash new items, particularly jeans – wash them on their own and usually in cold water because the colour will run and can wreck your other clothes.

READ THE LABELS

It's not rocket science but take it from someone who hates reading instructions of any sort and has paid the price with shrunken tees and never to be worn again shorts.

The labels can be easily found when you turn your clothes inside out. You might need to have a mummy look* as they can be evasive little buggers, but they are there, I promise!

*mummy look – this is the look you have when you actually want to find something. It involves opening one's eyes quite wide, being willing to move things around and turn things upside down. It requires commitment of longer than seven seconds and at 100% determination to achieve a positive result.

If the label says cold wash, then wash it in cold water, not warmish water, not hot water, not any degree in between – COLD!

If it says hand wash then I'm sorry but it really does mean get a bucket, add water and washing powder and put your delicate little hands into the bucket and squeeze and scrub. Then empty dirty water, add fresh water and do it all over again to rinse. Three times through should do it and then squeeze out excess water – yes by hand – and hang to dry.

I personally hate hand washing, almost as much as I hate cooking, but I have a really simple solution for you. Do not buy clothes that require hand washing. Check the labels when you are in the shop, or if you are online, read the fine print and make sure it can be thrown in a normal everyday wash just like everything else.

Other than the exceptions that I have already outlined above, you should be able to just throw your separate piles of whites and darks into a standard cycle in your machine.

THE 'B' WORD
(YES – BUDGETS)

I want to cry, and I'm sure reading this word makes you want to, too. I have put off writing this section to the point where there are almost no other sections left. My problem is that I love beautiful things. I love shiny new toys like the latest iPhone, iPad, i-anything. I love going on holidays and to Gold Class at the movies. I do not however, love anything that potentially restricts my access to these things. And for that reason, budgets can be challenging to make and for some people (like me), even harder to stick to.

As my kids can attest to, I banned the word hate in our house as they were growing up. Even brussels sprouts and mint peas were not to have this word used against them and I H.A.T.E both of them (not the kids, the brussels sprouts and peas). But now that they have left home I can say this out loud.

Unfortunately, budgets are a necessity. You need to learn how to manage your money so that you can pay your bills on time, as well as have cash leftover for the other things you need (or want). Side tip: learn the difference between what you *need* and what you *want.* I learnt early on to put my rent money aside as soon as I got paid. I also learnt the power of having a bank account that you can't access via an ATM at 2am on a drunken Sunday morning when you've run out of cash and your liver is screaming for a kebab.

Budgeting is a game of choice. CHOICE, not chance. You have to decide what is important to you and live within your means. If living out of home is important, then rent and bills have to take priority over top shelf spirits or designer clothes (unless of course you have a very well-paid job or trust fund – lucky you). If travelling overseas is on your bucket list, then you may have to ditch the bottomless brunches and takeaway lattes and settle for cornflakes and toast at home.

It's not about missing out, it's about adjusting your expectations and being willing to do what it takes to have the things that are important to you. That does not mean being willing to rob a bank in order to have it all, by the way. It means being patient and knowing that you don't have to do everything right now. Believe me, I know what it's like to want it now but I invite you to relax a little and remember you have a long life ahead of you and plenty of time to fit everything in.

SHOPPING FOR CLOTHES

I understand the importance of wanting to look good, particularly if you are single and trying to ensure that your Tinder pics are showing you at your best. Unless, of course, you are looking to hook up with someone who likes the grungy, hasn't-washed-for-a-week and doesn't-give-a-shit-about-how-he-looks kind of guy. You don't need designer clothes. Washing your hair every now and again and hanging your clothes up in your wardrobe as opposed to storing them in a crumpled pile on your floor, can do wonders to your overall appearance.

Keep your wardrobe simple – spend extra on a few items that you love and will wear to death and then pick up your basics from K-mart or somewhere similar. If designer labels are a must then take yourself off to the nearest op shop and checkout their racks. You can pick up some great items for less than a six-pack of cheap beer. And of course – hit the Boxing Day sales and the mid-year stock-take sales for other bargains.

If all else fails, you can always put clothes (or vouchers to your fave shops) onto your Christmas and birthday gift ideas lists. Better than the jocks and socks or a book about all the things you need to know about moving out of home, that you are likely to get instead.

SHOPPING FOR YOUR STOMACH

Being responsible for buying all your own food can be a little daunting. but I promise it can be managed in a way that will leave you plenty of money for going out.

I have a love-hate relationship with shopping lists. I love the idea of them and I really wished I used them properly because if I did, my pantry would not currently contain five packets of spiral pasta, four tins of tuna and two bottles of vinegar. Nor would we be using tissues instead of toilet paper because I was absolutely positive we had plenty of rolls left.

I hope that you will learn from my mistakes and take on using a list! And if you choose not to, that's fine, but I have a little warning for you – tissues just don't cut it with number twos.

ALDI = YOUR NEW BEST FRIEND

What ALDI may lack in brand selection, they make up for in bargains, with huge savings to be made on everything from meat, cheese and vegetables to your staples – milk, bread, rice, pasta and sauces.

And when it comes to toilet paper, laundry powder, detergents, cleaning products and tissues, ALDI is a must. These items are often much cheaper than in other major supermarkets.

And don't be afraid to try the different brands! Just because you don't recognise the packaging, doesn't mean it will taste bad.

THE OTHER SUPERMARKETS

I understand that ALDI is not for everyone and you may very well be attached to the mac and cheese brand that you've been eating since you were a toddler. Don't worry, you can still save money at these big chains as well but it will require a little extra thought. When you are standing in front of the 23 different types of bolognaise sauce on the shelf, it's easy for your eyes to glass over and for you to question whether you need sauce at all.

Finding the best value for money can be more difficult than getting the phone number of the cute assistant at the checkout. I mean how damn hard can they make it – different size jars, different prices and brands, some with parmesan, some with roasted veggies and some with nothing at all. You might need to try out a few of the cheaper options to see which taste better, but often the home brand ones taste pretty much the same as the fancy Paul Newman style brands.

Always look for specials. Sometimes these items are displayed at the end of the aisle and not in their usual spot. But beware, as just because they are at the end with huge "choose me, I'm special" banners flying above them, does not mean they are the cheapest. Check out the other brands in the aisle as well.

Compare the unit price of different sizes of the same brand as well as different brands. Look at the bottom of the price label. It tells you much you're paying per 100g, so this way you know how much bang your buck is getting.

Buying in bulk can be quite a lot cheaper but it can also be a trap, like if there is no way for you to get through 5kg of bacon before it's expiry date (no matter how much you love bacon). This is clearly not a problem for toilet paper – you can never have too much, and that's a fact.

Sometimes you can buy products loose or pre-packaged, e.g. nuts or salad mix – so check the prices on both.

GREEN = GOOD

All those years your parents spent trying to make you eat your veggies was not to fulfill some inner desire to torture you, it was to help ensure that you stay healthy and live long enough to provide them with grandkids. So do them a favour and throw in a few veggies once in a while.

Markets are a great option for fresh fruit and vegetables if you have one nearby. Frozen veggies last for months and months without going off, so keeping a supply in your freezer will keep Mum happy. You'll also save on wastage when you end up being out for dinner every night one week and the broccoli you bought now looks yellow instead of vibrant green.

MEAT

There is no requirement to become a vegetarian when you move out of home. If you want to, by all means go for it, but there are ways to keep meat in your diet without sacrificing social outings.

Buying in bulk is cheaper if you can manage it. Supermarkets are not always the cheapest or the best so it is worth keeping an eye out at the larger butcher shops for weekly specials.

If you make your slow cooker your new best friend, then you can get away with buying mega cheap cuts of meat. There is something special about placing chunks of meat into a pot and leaving it for 8-10 hours, only to return to melt-in-your-mouth meat.

SPICE IT UP

When it comes to herbs and spices, it's all about personal choice. If you can go fresh, great, but if not, just grab a jar or two from the supermarket.

My picks are; tuscan, garam masala, cajun, and mexican. Just sprinkle onto chicken, red meat or fish before cooking to create some variety without any additional work.

Plus there are a couple of must-haves (or at least they are in our kitchen) that I would recommend.

- Salt – I use sea salt or pink Himalayan salt because apparently they are better for you (or so I read or heard somewhere).
- Cracked pepper.
- Mixed herbs – the largest jar you can find as it can be added to pretty much anything and everything.

FOOD HYGIENE

Personal hygiene may not be top of your hygiene list unless you are trying to impress, however, hygiene in the kitchen is a must. Unless of course you are happy to roll the dice with getting salmonella poisoning.

The cause of several types of unwell-ness is food contamination. This means you have to take the time to prepare and cook your food safely. And I am not talking about sharp knives and fire from gas stoves. This is about avoiding bacteria – the painful, ugly, harmful type.

Here are some tips for helping to prevent various food poisoning:

- Cook meat and eggs thoroughly, no matter how much of a hurry you are in.

- Do not chop veggies or other food items on the same chopping board as you have used for raw meat, particularly chicken. Use plastic chopping boards for meat and always wash thoroughly afterwards with hot soapy water – and I do mean thoroughly.

- Hands need to be washed before and after handling raw foods.

- If it smells bad, it probably is – except when it's meant to smell bad, like blue cheese.

- Leftovers should always be eaten within three to four days of being cooked and should not be re-heated more than once.

- Food should be put into the fridge no more than two hours after it is cooked. The longer you leave it on the bench the greater the chance of bacteria growing on your food – gross!

- As a general rule, frozen food will keep in your freezer for about three months. If you haven't eaten it in this time then you probably aren't dying to eat it; throw it out.

TAKE-AWAY

- Yes, take-away can be expensive but there are going to be those days where you'd rather just hit the couch than face going into the kitchen. And that's ok, we all have them. If you live in a major city, then there are loads of options, not only including good old pizza, but also everybody's new best friend, UberEats.

- Noodle shops are a great (healthier) option if you don't mind leaving the couch to get it. Plus, if you add some extra veggies when you get home, one noodle box could probably feed two of you.

KITCHEN MUST-HAVES

Proper chefs will suggest doing everything from scratch and may even provide you with a long list of "essential" tools to have in your kitchen. When I started googling to see what these food gurus thought you should have in your kitchen, I couldn't decide whether to laugh or cry.

Here are just a few of the things I found:

Electric sharpener – my initial thought being what on earth do you need pencils for in the kitchen.

Sauté pan – a pan is a pan, don't you think?

A digital read instant thermometer is apparently a must, but considering I managed to keep a husband, two kids and numerous visitors fed for over 25 years not, I am not so sure.

And my all-time fave, a '*Benriner mandoline and an immersion blender*' – sounds too fancy for non-chefs to need.

But here's what you *actually* need…

THE BASICS

I might assume that you would know the basics already. However, I wouldn't be doing my job properly if I didn't cater for those of you that maybe don't know what basics are. You will need at least one each of the following. If you have any intention of having guests then you will need multiple, as BYO dishes doesn't really cut it.

- Dinner plate, bowl, side plate (for toast etc.)
- Knife, fork and spoons (soup/dessert and teaspoon)
- Glass
- Mug (for coffee/tea)
- Tea towels x 2
- Wine and/or champagne glass

GENERAL BITS AND PIECES

- Air-tight containers (great for leftovers)
- Microwave safe containers – get a few different sizes
- 1 x large mixing bowl
- Can opener
- Grater – don't go the cheapies as they rust too easily
- Measuring cups and spoons
- Tongs
- Egg flip
- Veggie peeler
- Plastic chopping board (best option for meat, particularly chicken)
- Wooden spoon
- Colander – aka strainer for pasta

KETTLE

Not much to say here. While most of your beverage consumption might be coming directly from the fridge and need only a bottle opener, you may also need that cup of liquid energy (aka coffee) to get you out the door each morning.

NON-STICK FRYPAN

Large and useful for cooking just about everything from bacon and eggs to stir-fry and steaks. Spend the money and get a good one or steal one from home. Only kidding, I meant "borrow" – for a very, very long time. It's also a good idea to not use steel spatulas or sharp knives in your "expensive" non-stick pan. They will destroy the surface and the non-stick magic will soon disappear.

You may think, like many a young man before you, that there is very little difference between non-stick frypans and "normal" frypans. I've heard the words "I'll just add oil or butter to make it non-stick" uttered too many times to count. Unfortunately oil and butter don't always cut it, so trust me – it's better to get the non-stick in the first place.

A SHARP KNIFE

Every kitchen should have a sharp, and I mean a really sharp, good quality knife. They should, in my opinion, come with a medical kit when you buy them but since they don't, I would also make sure you have one of those in close proximity to your kitchen. No matter how careful you are, a finger or two is bound to get sliced at some point in time, although as far as I am aware the stats on fingers being completely sliced off are pretty low!

BLENDER

Smoothies are a quick, healthy and easy brekky option; all you need is a good quality blender. There are a bucketload of Nutri Ninja's, Blitz's and Bullets (aka fruit crushing smoothie makers) currently on the market. The cheaper ones tend to have blades that don't do a great job, so spend a bit extra or get grandma to get you one for Christmas.

RICE COOKER

Everyone, including my own mother, tells me that cooking rice on the stovetop is easy. Maybe so but is it really easier than in a rice cooker. I mean, take one rice cooker, add rice, add water, flick switch and go watch TV while it does the work. No stirring, no stress about it boiling over. PLUS, it flicks itself to *keep warm* mode when done, so even if you forget about it, it won't turn into a blackened mess at the bottom of a pot, it will simply wait patiently for you to return.

The other bonus of rice is that it is cheap and filling. It can make pretty much any meal go much further - just add an extra cup or five of rice and you can feed an entire army.

As there are lots of different rice cookers out there, simply follow the instructions in the booklet that came with it. You will most likely find this booklet in the box, if you haven't thrown the box out already. If I'm too late and it's already long gone then it's pretty simple. For every 1 cup of white rice, add 1 ½ cups water and for brown rice add 2 ¼ cups water.

LARGE SLOW COOKER

You want to take advantage of cooking once and having enough leftovers for the following day, so a small one won't cut it.

For those of you who love meat but budget is a concern, this is the perfect option as you can buy the mega cheap cuts of meat and by the time they come out of the slow cooker, it is like they have been tenderized by some Greek god or goddess who has spent hours putting their heart and soul into making a gourmet masterpiece for you.

Your slow cooker may just become your new best mate. They don't make a huge mess, nor do they leave you with all the dishes (but I guess they *are* the dishes). They are happy to be left on their own all day and when you get home from work they greet you with mouth-watering aromas and a delicious meal, just waiting for you to put on a plate and devour. And what do they ask for in return? Not much really, just 10 minutes of attention in the morning, some fresh vegetables, some meat, a packet mix and some water.

Quick tip – most slow cooker recipes say to brown your meat first. If you're lazy like I am you can save some time and some dishes and skip this step. It made absolutely no difference and reduced the amount of effort I had to put in.

Plus, it doesn't matter if you and your housemates all need to eat at different times, your slow cooker can be switched to warm and left for those coming in late. Alternatively, you can put leftovers into microwave containers for easy reheating the next day.

JAFFLE MAKER

If you don't know what a jaffle maker is then you are most likely the child of a beautiful Italian or Greek Mumma who has spoiled you rotten with homemade to-die-for meals and treats, all made from scratch of course. It's probably no surprise that my own son has a lot of mates from these cultures. He is smart of course – what growing teen boy wouldn't want to spend time with motherly types who express their love in the form of large plates of deliciousness. Thankfully I am not insecure as a mother. I know they love me for who I am. Don't you guys?

A jaffle maker (also known as a toasted sandwich press) is the most versatile piece of kitchen machinery invented. You can make breakfast, lunch and dinner in this little beauty. Banana and cinnamon for brekky, the standard ham, cheese and tomato for lunch and leftover anything filling for dinner. But more ideas later.

OTHER HOUSEHOLD ESSENTIALS

I've talked about kitchen essentials up to now because I know how important managing the needs of your stomach is. However, there are a few other things you need in your new home.

- First-Aid Kit
- Washing basket
- Pegs
- Screwdriver – I do not mean the drink
- Scissors
- Spare batteries for things like TV remotes and clocks
- Fire extinguisher

IMPRESSING THAT
VERY SPECIAL SOMEONE

So, you might not be the best cook on the planet. So what! That does not mean that you can't impress the pants off that special someone.

Dinner for two can be simple, romantic and doesn't have to cost the earth. It is, however, advisable that you get rid of your housemates for the evening.

AMBIANCE

This is a fancy word which actually means the following:

- Clean your house and remove all evidence of an all-guy household.

- Now clean again as I'm sure you missed things the first time round.

- Scented candles – simple, beautiful, romantic and can disguise even the most revolting of stale, manly odours.

- Try a picnic rug on the floor in the lounge instead. If you have a fireplace – even better! This way you can go with paper plates and still look cool.

- Nice music, and I do NOT mean head banging, retro, dance, heavy metal or rock. You don't have to resort to Michael Bublé if that's not your thing. But choose something simple that can be going in the background while you chat, eat or do whatever it is that you will doing during the evening.

THE FOOD

I am a strong believer of the KISS principle: Keep It Simple, Stupid. You don't want to spend the entire evening in the kitchen. You want something that can be prepared earlier so you get to hang out together as much as possible. Here are some ideas to get you started:

HOMEMADE PIZZAS

Find out what your date's favourite toppings are beforehand. You can buy great pizza bases already made up, and just add more of whatever toppings you want. They can be done earlier in the day and kept in the fridge, ready to go in the oven when you want them. This is perfect for the picnic in the lounge option.

QUICHE AND SALAD

Buy a pre-made quiche from your local deli. Go for something a little fancier than the normal bacon and cheese variety – maybe try pumpkin and feta.

As for salad, go for mixed leaves rather than plain lettuce and add some crushed seeds/nuts, cherry tomatoes, thinly sliced mango or apple and a simple dressing (lemon juice, seeded mustard and olive oil works well, or you can go for a bottled dressing from the supermarket).

By the way, quiche isn't a threat to your masculinity, in case you've been led to believe that like many men before you. But if you are not a quiche fan, that's cool, you'll find some other ideas in the Fast 5 recipes section at the back of this book.

GETTING THE MOST OUT OF VISITING HOME

Here are my three tips for ultimate success when visiting the people who raised you:

1. Do not take your washing home! They have spent more than 18 years washing your dirty jocks and socks – they deserve a break. Take bunch of flowers instead. You don't have to spend any money, just discretely pick some from your neighbour's garden or from the side of the road. Your loved-one won't even notice if they are wilted or weed-like, because of how thoughtful the gesture is.

2. Don't make them resort to begging or bribing in order to have you come visit. They miss you! Call out of the blue and ask if you can come for dinner. You know it can be last minute, but if you want that homemade apple crumble with that vanilla bean ice-cream you love so much, then give them a bit of notice!

3. Ask about their day/week/life. While you may not realise it, they do have one, and since you left home, it no longer revolves completely around you. Try to listen (and be interested) in what they say. I know that lunch with their friends or what is happening at work are not at the top, or probably even the bottom, of your list of interests, but give it a go.

Once you have lived out of home for a while you will start to realise how much your parents did for you that you never really noticed – paying the electricity bills, keeping the internet going, unblocking drains… Make sure that you thank them and tell them how much you appreciate them.

They don't expect this because they remember what it was like to be your age, but they will appreciate it none the less. Call them every now and again to say hi because while they may have converted your bedroom into a theatre room or gym, they really do miss you.

WHO GETS THE X-BOX – EXITING YOUR SHARE HOUSE

There are many reasons why you may want (or need) to leave your share house haven. The *friends* you moved in with may have turned out to be completely insane. Perhaps they still think that mop is just another name for a small, fluffy dog. Maybe they thought that having their girlfriend stay over 6 nights per week, every week, without chipping in for bills was ok. Or maybe your circumstances have changed – a new partner, a change of job, an increase or decrease in your income or a decision to travel the world for a year or two or forever. Or maybe you just missed your mum – it's okay, you don't need to admit it out loud. We get it. Either way, there is some stuff to manage.

Firstly, you're going to want your share of the bond back. If the rest of your roomies are happy to continue with the lease then a replacement for you will need to be found and this is your responsibility. If they already have someone who wants to move in (like the girl who has been staying there for a year already without paying any rent) then sweet – she can pay you directly.

If not, then it's time for you and your roomies to put on ad onto one of the many online share house sites and start interviewing prospective replacements.

The right thing to do is to pay rent until the new you has been found and can move in, unless you and your roomies have made a different agreement.

When you move out, make sure that your bedroom is left clean for the new you. That doesn't mean just take your stuff, it means vacuum, dust, clean the leftover blue tack off the walls and if necessary shampoo the carpet in your room. It is not fair for the new you to have to deal with the smell of stale beer and 12-day-old pizza crusts.

As for the rest of the house – be fair. Clean out the fridge, get rid of your rubbish and do a general tidy up of the common areas as well.

There may also be some big-ticket items that you all chipped in to buy, you know, the stuff you maybe couldn't afford on your own - a fridge, washing machine or maybe even a big screen TV. So who gets what? You can't split a TV in half, now can you? This is a conversation that you perhaps should have had when you first made those group purchases, but oh well, it looks like you're having it now.

I'm keeping my fingers crossed for you that the decision to move out has not been because of a falling out, and that you are all still good mates. If so, then easy peasy – just have a chat and come to an agreement about who gets what and if need be, who needs to buy out the other.

If remaining mates is as likely as committing to a life of celibacy and negotiation is not possible, then you may have to say goodbye to that item and your share of it. Sometimes the peace you will achieve by moving out of a place that no longer works for you, will be more valuable than the money you may have lost in the process. But I truly hope it doesn't come to that.

As for the other bits and pieces you bought to the house – what's yours is yours. If you bought the microwave, then take it. Same for pots and pans, cutlery, laundry baskets and even the pegs if you really want them.

My advice when it comes to group purchases is – don't! Regardless of how the relationships end up, it is just difficult to deal with in a way that's fair to all involved.

Buy cheaper second hand if need be and/or have something in writing about who takes what when you all split. It's bound to happen one day as I'm pretty sure your future partners are not going to be very keen about raising the kids in a share house with your mates taking up the prime couch spot and constantly leaving the toilet seat up.

A FINAL WORD OR TWO
(OK - MAYBE THREE)

As my kids would tell you, I am not a woman of few words. I generally have a lot to say which I'm sure is the cause of more than one or two eye rolls. However, I would like to think that some of my advice has been a help to them as they ventured out into the big wide world on their own.

Moving out is a big thing but it doesn't have to be stressful or scary. It's just another "first", and you have actually survived plenty of "firsts" in your life up to this point. Things that you haven't done before, things that you had no idea you could do – and more often than not you not only survived, but you nailed them. Learning to ride a bike, drive a car, sitting exams, starting your first job or travelling on your own. This is just another in a long list of firsts that will contribute to making your life the big adventure that it should be.

And if you aren't ready to take the plunge just yet, that's cool too. Settle into the couch and enjoy that home cooking for a bit longer. Trust me, they won't mind one bit. Unless of course you are approaching 30 and then, seriously dude, it's time to get on your bike.

Enjoy the ride.

(Keep reading for Fast 5 Recipe ideas.)

FAST 5 RECIPES

FAST 5 RECIPES

If you have opened the pages of this chapter expecting an outpouring of incredible recipes straight from the heart of my kitchen, you are about to be shattered because in case you haven't caught on yet, I would do anything that gets me far *far* away from a kitchen. I can't even watch shows like My Kitchen Rules or MasterChef as they make me feel like a small child about to get into trouble for not turning the beaters off before licking the chocolate icing off them. I mean, do people really make everything from scratch?

And what's so horrific about a packet mix anyway?

It's all about keeping things easy for you. Great meal options do not have to mean hard work and bucketloads of time. And if you love to cook then go for the start-from-scratch options in any of these recipes. And if you're not doing anything on the weekend, feel free to pop over and cook for me.

But for those of you who need a helping hand, I have scoured the world (actually just my good mate Google, and my own mother) for a handful of great recipes to help keep you alive long enough to find a partner and give your mother grand-children.

I have fondly called this my "Fast 5" selection – inspired by how fast I like to get in, and out, of the kitchen when I cook.

EGGS EVERY WAY

I am starting with eggs because whether they are fried, poached, scrambled, omeletted or boiled, they are one of the easiest and most versatile meal options on the planet (unless of course you are vegan, in which case, skip this section). However, you'd be surprised (or maybe not) how many people do not know how to boil an egg, let alone poach one so here you go.

All eggs, with the exception of boiled, are best served immediately. Boiled eggs can be stored in the fridge as a handy snack on their own or to be added to salads.

BOILED

Fill a pot with enough cold water to cover your eggs by about 2cm. Place over medium heat. For soft-boiled eggs, simmer for four minutes and for hard boiled simmer for eight minutes.

SCRAMBLED

Break two eggs into a bowl (no shells). Beat with a fork, add a little milk. Heat your pan to medium, add a little butter and then pour in your eggs. Use a spatula to fold continuously (sort of like mixing) until they look cooked. Don't overcook them or you could end up with dry rubbery eggs, as opposed to the nice fluffy ones you were hoping for.

OMELETTE

Exactly the same as for scrambled but no folding. Once the egg mixture is in the pan, add your favourite toppings (see list below) to one half of the omelette. Once the filling has been adding, lift one side of the omelette and fold it over the side with the filling to enclose it.

FRIED

Crack egg/s into frying pan with a little butter or oil. Cook until the clear parts of the egg have turned white. If you like hard yolks then flip your egg over and cook further. Otherwise leave them sunny side up which means yolks facing up.

POACHED

Fill saucepan ¾ full with water and boil. Add a teaspoon of vinegar if you have any as it can help the egg hold its shape. Reduce heat to low. Crack egg into small measuring cup and then carefully slide the egg into your saucepan. Cook for four minutes. Use a spoon with holes in it to remove your egg from the water otherwise you'll end up with soggy toast.

TOPPINGS & SIDES

Toast, avocado, fresh or dried tomatoes, mushrooms, spinach, cheese of any sort, hollandaise sauce, bacon, salmon.

BREAKFASTS

There are generally two types of people – morning people and not morning people. The latter group can be easily identified by their 'don't even think about talking to me before coffee' scowl on their face. This group is the most likely to skip breakfast entirely, that is if they make it out of bed before noon. However for those of you who are fortunate enough to be morning people, here are some breakfast alternatives to toast and vegemite or muesli.

BACON & EGG MUFFIN (MINUS THE MACCAS)

Ronnie McD is not the only one who can knock together a mean brekky muffin – here is an easy DIY version you can do at home.

INGREDIENTS
1 egg (fried or poached)
2 rashes bacon
1 English muffin
Cheese
Sauce (if desired)

STEPS
1. Fry your bacon (if you don't want to cook up bacon, use ham).
2. Cook egg the way you like it best (see instructions above).
3. Toast muffin.
4. Add bacon, egg and other toppings. Put on lid and eat!

BANANA BERRY SMOOTHIE

It doesn't get any simpler than this. Chuck it all in, hit a button, pour and go. For those of you who literally need to eat on the run, invest in a drink container with a good lid and easy access drinking capabilities. Note, spilling a smoothie in your car is a nightmare that will haunt you for weeks. The stale milk smell is almost impossible to get rid of and liquid tends to get into cracks that you never even knew existed in your car. As for spilling on public transport – pure embarrassment.

INGREDIENTS
1 banana
1 cup frozen (or fresh) berries (blue, strawb, rasp or black)
Milk
Yoghurt
2-3 ice cubes (leave out if using frozen berries)

OPTIONAL DEPENDING ON PERSONAL TASTE
Honey, cinnamon, rolled oats (for a more substantial brekky)

STEPS
1. Put everything in a blender.
2. Hit the on switch.
3. Blend until zero lumps then drink.

PANCAKES

While not super-fast, this family fave had to go on the list. To speed it up you can buy pancake mixture already made up from the supermarket – it's in the same aisle as the flour.

INGREDIENTS
1 egg (fried or poached)
1 cup self-raising flour
1 cup milk
Pinch of salt

STEPS
1. Put all of the ingredients into a blender.
2. Mix on high until it is all combined.
3. Heat some butter in a large frying pan and pour in some mixture.
4. When you see little bubble appearing, flip them over.
5. Cook for a little longer, then remove from pan.
6. Repeat until all your mixture is gone.
7. Add your favourite toppings – berries, bananas, lemon & sugar, ice-cream, maple syrup…

MUFFINS

This option will take you a little time and I recommend you tackle them on a weekend or one evening rather than getting your butt out of bed early enough of a morning to cook a batch. The best thing about these is once you have made them, you can put them in an airtight container and brekky is done for a few days or you can freeze them and have them as a backup brekky for later. This recipe makes 12 but you can always double it to make more.

INGREDIENTS
2 cups self-raising flour
½ cup sugar
1 egg beaten
¼ cup oil
1 cup milk

STEPS
1. Put all of the ingredients in a bowl.
2. Mix until just combined.
3. Add your own flavourings (ideas below).
4. Bake at 180C for about 20 minutes.

Here are a few muffin flavour suggestions but go nuts and experiment with a few of your own.

Mashed banana and Nutella
Diced apple and ground cinnamon
Fresh raspberries/blueberries with oats and a dash of honey

BANANA SPLIT – THE HEALTHY WAY

Your mum doesn't have to stress about you eating dessert for breakfast with this fun but healthy option.

INGREDIENTS
1 banana
½ cup yoghurt (you pick the flavor)
¼ cup muesli
¼ cup berries (you pick which sort)

STEPS
1. Split the banana lengthways and put in bowl.
2. Add yoghurt.
3. Top with muesli and your berries.

LUNCH

I'm a bit of a sandwich, wrap, salad or soup kind of girl when it comes to lunches. I'm out and about so it means I either pick up a bite at a local café or I bring my lunch with me from home. If you are on a budget, which you most likely will be, then you might need these simple take-anywhere lunch ideas.

LAZY LEFTOVERS

A truly brilliant option for lunches which requires no real work at all is to make enough for dinner the night before so you have leftovers for lunch. Nearly anything can be lunch-boxed, but some good options include:

Pasta
Risotto
Slow cooker meals
Roast meats and veggies – either on their own and added to a wrap
Stir fry noodles

SUPER SANDWICHES & WRAPS

Easy peasy right! All you need is a loaf of bread (or packet of wraps), your favourite toppings, some glad wrap (or airtight lunch container) and el cheapo lunch is a done deal.

When buying bread, I recommend staying away from bakery loaves as they tend to go stale much quicker than the supermarket options. My personal preference is the Helga's varieties as they are substantial, have a great range to suit all tastes and last 5-7 days.

Sandwich toppings are easy – no doubt you are cool with vegemite, peanut butter and the toppings that made it regularly to your school lunchbox. However now that you are making your own lunches, you might like to be a little more adventurous so below are a few new lunchbox ideas for you.

Bacon, avocado, lettuce, tomato and mayonnaise
Turkey or Ham with avocado, feta, spinach
Falafel with sun dried tomatoes, mixed lettuce, red onion, and hummus
Tuna (in spring water) with sweet corn, capsicum, tomato, cucumber and lettuce
Ham, cheese and Dijon mustard
Chicken, pesto, lettuce
Chorizo, red capsicum and salsa
Roast beef and coleslaw

PIMPED UP 2-MINUTE NOODLES

I am not a fan of 2-minute noodles, even though I have succumbed to their quick and cheap appeal at times. But if you are going to go there, you may as well go there in style with these super simple noodle veggie cups. This recipe makes 6 but feel free to double it.

INGREDIENTS
170 g Maggi 2-minute noodles, chicken flavoured
3 cups grated mixed vegetables (your choice)
2 eggs lightly beaten
½ cup sour cream
½ cup chopped ham (optional of course)
½ cup tasty cheese
Tomato salsa (the jar variety is perfect)

STEPS
1. Preheat oven to 180 degrees C.
2. Grease a six-muffin pan with oil.
3. Cook noodles as it says on the packet but keep flavour sachets aside. Drain then rinse under cold water then place into a bowl.
4. Add the flavour sachets, grated vegetables, egg, sour cream and ham and mix.
5. Spoon mixture into muffin pan and top with grated cheese.
6. Bake for 30-35 minutes.
7. Serve warm with tomato salsa.

SPICY CHICKEN GUACAMOLE BOWLS

A healthy, chuck-it-all-in-a-bowl lunch option for those wanting a little more spice in their day.

INGREDIENTS
3 cups cooked brown or white rice
1 medium cucumber
1 medium carrot
1/4 bunch coriander
1 cup snow peas
BBQ chicken – chopped (can use cooked fillets instead if you prefer)
1 cup guacamole (150gm)
4 Tablespoon sriracha (chilli sauce)

STEPS
1. Dice the cucumber, grate carrot and roughly chop the coriander.
2. Place 1 cup of cooked rice in a bowl or lunch container.
3. Mix all other ingredients together and then add to top of rice.
4. Drizzle the sriracha/chilli sauce over top.

ZUCCHINI SLICE

Do not put this book down just because the title of this recipe has a green veggie in it. Do not skip to the next recipe. Please do yourself a favour and at least give this one a go. I have included it because it is ridiculously simple, filling, and it has bacon in it. Plus you can make a large tray of it and have lunch all sorted for a few days.

INGREDIENTS
5 eggs
1 cup self-raising flour, sifted if possible
375g zucchini, grated
1 large onion, finely chopped
200g rindless bacon, chopped
1 cup grated cheese
1/4 cup vegetable oil

STEPS
1. Preheat oven to 170 degree C.
2. Beat the eggs in a large bowl until combined then add the flour. Beat until smooth, then throw in everything else and stir until combined.
3. Grease and line (with grease proof paper) a 30 x 20cm ovenproof casserole dish or cake tin.
4. Pour your mixture into the tin and bake in oven for 30 minutes or until cooked through.

DINNER

I know budget can be a big factor in determining what to cook for dinner but one cannot live on 2 minute noodles alone, although I have seen some people give it a red hot go. So maybe mix it up a little. Splurge on a steak once in a while if that's your thing. Or organic veggies. Or lobster. Ok, maybe not lobster, but you get my drift.

SPAG BOL

If I was to be honest about the best way to achieve perfect pasta, I would suggest you ask someone else as I'm a tad on the hit and miss side. It's not that my pasta is ever BAD, but *al dente* could be a small village in the south of Italy for all I know.

The only tip I've got for you is to add some salt to your water and then make sure it is really boiling before you add your pasta. Stir every now and again to stop it sticking to bottom of pan. I always use Angel Hair spaghetti (the really thin one) as it only takes 2-3 minutes to cook!

Everyone needs a quick easy spag bol at some point in their life. For the men in my family, this means once a week at least. There are hundreds of different recipes out there and you can go from scratch, jar or a mixture of the two. Here's just one option but experiment till you get the best 'bol' for your soul, or at least your stomach.

INGREDIENTS

1 tablespoon olive oil

1 medium brown onion, finely chopped

2 medium carrot, peeled, grated

2 garlic cloves, crushed (from a jar is fine)

500g beef mince

1 jar of your favourite tomato based pasta sauce

1 teaspoon oregano or mixed herbs

500g thin spaghetti (quicker to cook but any pasta is ok)

Grated cheese and/or parmesan

Parmesan

STEPS

1. Heat oil in a large saucepan over medium-high heat. Cook onion, carrot and garlic, stirring until softened. Add mince. Cook until mince is browned.
2. Add tomato based sauce, oregano/mixed herbs and ½ cup cold water. Bring to the boil. Reduce heat to low and simmer, uncovered for 20-30 minutes or until the sauce thickens.
3. Cook pasta in a separate large saucepan of boiling, salted water. Follow directions on packet for details about cooking time. Once cooked, drain.
4. Dish up pasta, pour sauce over top.
5. Serve with parmesan and/or grated cheese.

Bolognaise might not be your thing but there is no limit to what you can add to this quick, cheap and easy staple. Keep it plain with a spoonful or two of pesto (yes, the jar variety is fine) or add your veggies of choice with your sauce of choice. Plus make extra and lunch (or dinner) the next day is all sorted.

CHICKEN PARMIE

A Parmie does not have to be reserved for pub nights. They are a favourite of nearly all the men I know so I thought they deserved their spot at number one in my Fast 5 dinners. This recipe makes four parmies so why not get the mates over, add a beer or two and settle in for a night at home.

INGREDIENTS
1 jar tomato-based pasta sauce
4 crumbed chicken breasts (available from deli)
4 slices leg ham
1 ½ cups grated cheese (the mixed cheese varies in supermarket are a tasty option)
Olive oil
Mixed herbs (optional)

STEPS
1. Heat oven to 200 degrees C (180 degrees C fan forced). Line a baking tray with baking paper.
2. Heat olive oil in a frying pan over medium heat. Add crumbed chicken breasts and cook for 3 minutes on each side. You may need to cook in batches depending on size of frying pan.
3. Remove chicken once cooked and place onto tray with baking paper.
4. Top with tomato sauce then ham. Spread cheese over the top. Bake for 15 minutes or until cheese is completely melted.
5. Serve with veggies or salad.

FULLY LOADED BAKED POTATOES

Looking for total ease and flexibility with your meal? This is the option for you. You can top these baked spuds with whatever you have in your fridge at the time or get as creative as you want. No rules.

INGREDIENTS
4 large washed potatoes
Plus toppings of your choice (some ideas below):

Baked beans (canned black beans or chilli beans)
Bacon, finely chopped
Minced beef (cook with Taco seasoning for Mexican vibe)
Veggies – onions, corn, mushrooms, red peppers, tomatoes, avocado
Chopped chives (or other herbs of your choice)
Cheese – tasty/feta/cottage
Sauces - sour cream/salsa/barbeque/tomato/sweet chilli/pesto

STEPS
1. Preheat oven to 200 degrees C.
2. Using a fork, pierce (aka stab) the potatoes in about 6 places as this helps them cook faster.
3. Place them onto the oven rack in centre of oven. You can put them in baking tray if you prefer. Bake for 50 to 60 minutes or until tender when a skewer is inserted into the centre.
4. Cut a deep cross in top of each potato. Squeeze base gently to open.
5. Add your choice of topping and serve.

FRIED RICE

In the spirit of KISS – Keep It Simple, Stupid, here is my no-fail fried rice. The perfect side dish or on its own as a main meal.

INGREDIENTS
1 tablespoon oil
1 teaspoon minced garlic
½ medium onion, chopped
3 medium carrots, diced
1 cup cooked roast chicken (shredded or diced) or bacon or other meat of your choice
1 cup frozen peas (or any frozen veggie mix)
1 cup broccoli, chopped
3-4 cups cooked rice (for best result use rice that has been cooked and cooled already but this is not a deal breaker).
2 tablespoons oyster sauce
2 tablespoons soy sauce
salt & pepper

STEPS
1. Preheat oil in a wok or large frying pan (medium heat).
2. Add carrots, stir and cook for two minutes. Add garlic and onions, cooking for another two minutes.
3. Add chopped meat, peas and rice and stir.
4. Add in the oyster and soy sauces. Stir constantly until rice is coated with sauce and all ingredients are heated thoroughly. Add more oil if the rice starts to stick at all.
5. Add salt and pepper and serve.

OVEN BAKED PUMPKIN RISOTTO

I don't know many people who don't love a good risotto. But I do know plenty that hate making it (me included) because it is so incredibly time consuming. But there is an easier way.

INGREDIENTS
½ butternut pumpkin (chopped into small cubes)
10g butter
2 tablespoons olive oil
1 teaspoon minced garlic (or 2 cloves crushed)
1 ½ cups arborio rice
4 ½ cups chicken stock
1 cup grated parmesan cheese
2 tablespoons parsley (fresh if possible)
40g unsalted butter to add at the end
Salt and cracked black pepper

STEPS
1. Preheat oven to 180 degrees C.
2. Heat a non-stick frying pan over medium heat. Add the butter, oil, garlic, and pumpkin and cook for 5 minutes, then add the parsley.
3. Place the rice, stock, and pumpkin mixture in a large baking dish and stir until combined. Sprinkle with salt and pepper.
4. Cover tightly with foil. Bake for 40 minutes or until most of the liquid is absorbed. Remove from oven, stir in parmesan and 40g butter.
5. Add extra salt and pepper depending on your personal taste.
6. Serve straight away.

VARIATIONS
Not everyone is a fan of pumpkin. My grandfather used to say it was cow food which didn't stop my mother forcing it upon me as a child. As I have grown older and wiser and my taste buds have died off a little, I have come to like it. But if you have not, don't despair, because here are some great alternatives that you can easily swap them out for:

Chicken and Leek
2 x chicken fillets, chopped into small pieces and 1 x leek, finely sliced). I often add sundried tomatoes to this option as well.

Mushroom
200g sliced mushrooms

Chorizo and cauliflower
1-2 chorizo sausages – sliced, and ½ medium chopped cauliflower

Don't be afraid to experiment with other ingredients including zucchini, tomatoes, bacon, tuna, spinach, basil and lemons.

SWEET TREATS

We all need a little sweetness in our lives every now and again. Forget the sugar-free, guilt-free options and try out one of my Fast 5.

CARAMEL BANANAS

With only 3 ingredients you can't go wrong with this simple but oh so yummy dessert.

INGREDIENTS
1 banana
2 tablespoons butter
2 tablespoons brown sugar

STEPS
1. Melt butter in frying pan over medium heat. Add brown sugar and mix until dissolved. Add chopped bananas and cook for 2-3 minutes until bananas are soft.
2. Serve with cream or ice-cream.

CHOCOLATE BROWNIES

I don't think there is anyone on the planet who doesn't love a chocolate brownie. And if there is, it just means even more for you.

INGREDIENTS
250g butter
2 cups caster sugar
4 eggs
1 ½ cups plain flour
¾ cup cocoa
1 teaspoon vanilla essence

STEPS
1. Preheat oven to 180 degrees C. Line a 20 x 30cm baking tin with non-stick baking paper.
2. Melt butter in a saucepan over medium heat. Remove from heat and stir in the sugar. Add the eggs, 1 at a time, and stir until mixture is thick and shiny.
3. Sift the flour and cocoa powder, add to the egg mixture and mix well. Add the vanilla and stir.
4. Pour mixture into your baking tin. Make sure it is spread evenly.
5. Bake for 30 minutes or until a skewer inserted into the middle comes out clean. Leave in the pan until it has cooled completely.
6. Serve on its own or with cream or ice-cream.

MA'S APPLE CRUMBLE

My son would kill me if I didn't include his absolute favourite to the list. While it breaks my heart just a little to admit, he does prefer my mother's apple crumble over mine, so here it is.

INGREDIENTS
Large tin of pie apples
1 cup plain flour
60g butter
½ cup white or brown sugar
1 teaspoon cinnamon or allspice (optional)

STEPS
1. Preheat oven to 200 degrees C.
2. In a medium bowl, rub the butter and flour together using your finger tips to form small pieces, then add the sugar (and cinnamon/allspice) and mix to form the crumble.
3. Put the apples in the bottom of a baking dish and add the crumble mixture on top.
4. Bake for 15-20 minutes or until brown on top.
5. Serve with cream or ice-cream or both.

CHOCOLATE RIPPLE CAKE

Simple but impressive.

INGREDIENTS
500ml thickened cream
1 teaspoon caster sugar
1 teaspoon vanilla essence
250gm packet Choc Ripple biscuits
Fresh berries

STEPS
1. Beat the cream, sugar and vanilla in a bowl. Use an electric beater if you have one.
2. Spread a little cream along the bottom of a serving plate and then spread cream on each biscuit. Sandwich them together to make one long biscuit log.
3. Spread the rest of the cream over the top of the log. Cover and put in fridge for a few hours to set.
4. Add fresh berries or grated chocolate before serving. Or both!

SMASHED PAV (AKA ETON MESS)

This traditional English dessert is popular all over the world and with only four ingredients needed to create this tasty little mess, will be kind on your budget. While you can serve in bowls, it is super impressive in glasses instead.

INGREDIENTS
200g mixed berries
4 x meringue nests (buy from supermarket)
150ml thickened cream
2 teaspoons honey

STEPS
1. Place the berries in a bowl and crush with the back of a fork.
2. Spoon half into four bowls or glasses.
3. Add ½ of the crushed meringue nests.
4. Mix the cream and honey together in a small bowl.
5. Add the remaining crushed fruit and stir until just combined.
6. Add to your four bowls and then top with remaining crushed meringue and some extra berries.
7. Serve immediately.

THE FINAL FINAL WORD

So if you didn't find anything you liked in my Fast 5, no problem. There's this little thing, some of you might know it, called the Internet. It is overflowing with great recipes to suit any level of fussiness (I mean taste) and budget. Not to mention step by step YouTube clips to guide you through everything from poached eggs to crème brulee.

For that matter, try googling "when house-cleaning sucks, how can you make it fun" – you'll be surprised at how many people have posted videos about this topic. Please note, I'm not saying what you find will actually be of any help, but they might give you a bit of a laugh while you are avoiding cleaning that bathroom.

And if all else fails, there are older, wiser family members you can call for advice. They will love the opportunity to help you out, as well as to say hi and see how you are doing.

So from me and guardians all over, good luck, well done, and eat your veggies.